www.DrKelleyPendleton.com

ISBN: 1512362425

ISBN 13: 978-1512362428

Disclaimer:

This workbook is designed and intended solely to provide information to its readers and is not an exhaustive discussion of the content area. The information is provided with the understanding that the author or publisher are not engaged to render any type of legal, accounting, business, financial, tax or any other kind of professional advice or services. No warranties or guarantees of any kind including those concerning local, state, or professional legality, marketing success, financial growth, or practice growth are expressed or implied. Neither the publisher nor the individual author shall be held liable or responsible to any person or entity for any injuries, losses, untoward results, physical, mental, emotional, financial, economic, commercial, or character damages, including, but not limited to, special, incidental, indirect, consequential, punitive or other damages which are or are perceived to be the result of any actions taken or inspired by the information supplied in this workbook. The reader alone is responsible for his or her own decisions, choices, actions, and results. Every healthcare business and practitioner is different and the information and strategies contained herein may not be suitable for your situation. Please consult with an appropriate and qualified legal, accounting, business, financial, or tax professional for advice specific to your situation.

Welcome!

Thank you for purchasing the companion workbook to **Community Connections!** *Relationship Marketing for Healthcare Professionals.* In this workbook, we'll delve deeper into some of the issues and topics discussed in the *Community Connections!* book. I hope, as you work through this workbook, you'll reach a greater understanding of yourself, your practice, your communities – and the interrelationship of all three. Once you begin leveraging your Community Connections, you can create the practice – and life – of your dreams!

A few thoughts before we begin:

- You'll find this workbook is organized into sections that reflect the parts and chapters of **Community Connections!** It's not necessary to work through the sections in order…go at your own pace and do what feels right.

- Please be **brutally honest** when answering the questions in this workbook. No one but you will see your responses, and you'll receive maximal impact and clarity if you're totally honest. (You'll get *out* of it what you put *into* it.)

- Some of the questions in this workbook may make you uncomfortable. Overcome the urge to skip those questions, because often what we most need to work through makes us uncomfortable. It's been said if you're comfortable you're not growing.

- Please be thorough and comprehensive in your answers. The more detailed responses you give…the deeper you dig…the more you'll get out of this workbook.

- If you're part of a Mastermind Group, some of these workbook questions could be posed to the group to promote discussion. (If you've never heard of a Mastermind Group before, please refer to Chapter 7 of **Community Connections!)**

- Stay focused. We usually have most of the answers we need in our own heads…we just need a quiet space, someone to ask the right questions, and the strength to answer honestly and completely. Finally, we must be willing to put in the time and do the work to create the practice and life of our dreams!

As always, I wish you much success in your life and career. If you have a success story to share, please email me at DrKelley@DrKelleyPendleton.com. I look forward to creating a larger healthcare marketing community with you!

Part 1:
Where to Begin?

Chapter 1: Why Don't Healthcare Professionals "Market?"

1. **What's your experience in business, marketing, practice management, et cetera? (Include natural aptitudes, classes, life experience, workshops, and anything else that's relevant.)**

2. **What are your feelings and emotions about marketing your practice?**

3. Where do you think your feelings and emotions about marketing come from?

4. Why don't you market your practice...OR...why don't you market your practice in the way you think you should? (Select all that apply!)

- □ I'm good at what I do. Isn't that enough?

- □ Yikes – It's scary!

- □ I'm a shy/reserved sort of person.

- □ I don't have time.

- □ I don't have a budget for marketing.

- □ I'm exhausted just running my practice.

- □ I don't know how.

- □ Other: _____

- □ Other: _____

5. **What do you perceive to be barriers to your effective marketing?**

6. **What suggestions would you make to a colleague with the same perceived barriers to effective marketing?**

7. **As an educated healthcare provider, you're obviously good at what you do…why isn't that enough to produce a successful practice?**

8. **It can be hard to market yourself. Putting yourself "out there" can make you feel vulnerable. How can you mitigate this anxiety?**

9. **What is the scariest or hardest component of marketing for you? How would you advise a friend to get past this fear or issue?**

10. **What are some marketing strategies you could use even if you're painfully shy?**

11. How can you free up time in your day?

12. Write down everything you do for the next 3-7 days. Look for time robbers and ways to consolidate your efforts. How much time can you free up?

13. What have you done in the past to market your practice for less than $100? Less than 250? What were the results?

14. How can you increase your energy? How can you avoid burnout? List 25 things you love to do – that can give you energy – that cost less than $10.

15. What are you most passionate about and why? How can you incorporate these passions into your practice?

16. Have you ever had someone say they wish they'd known about you, your services, or your products sooner? Describe the situation and how it made you feel.

14

17. Do you know people who could benefit from your services or products – or professionals who could refer people to you – but they don't understand what you do? Who?

18. How can you increase your marketing know-how?

19. **Who are your past and current mentors? What about them do you most respect? What have they taught you? What did / can they help you with?**

20. **List at least 3 people you would like to have as your mentor and why. Do you know him/her? Do you know someone who can make an introduction?**

21. Who could you be a mentor to? (What are your biggest strengths, and who could benefit from them?)

22. What's included and excluded in your state's scope of practice?

23. Do you feel your scope of practice is adequate, or does it need to be updated? If you think it should be updated, what do you think needs to change?

24. Imagine you were barely marketing your practice at all. What would that look like? What would it feel like? How would your life be different?

25. Imagine you were marketing your practice to your full potential. What would that look like? What would it feel like? How would your life be different?

Chapter 2: Do You Know Who You Are?

1. How would you (or people who know you well) describe your personality?

2. What is your professional identity or reputation?

3. How would you (or people who know you well) describe your *professional* personality?

4. What is your professional purpose?

5. List the top 5 things you're most passionate about. Brainstorm ways in which you could incorporate each into your daily practice.

6. In what ways is your personal lifestyle congruent with your profession? For example, if you're a dentist and you floss twice a day. (List 5-10)

7. **In what ways is your personal lifestyle *incongruent* with your profession? For example, you tell your patients not to smoke, but you do. (List 5-10)**

8. **Of your areas of incongruence, which ones are most directly linked to your profession? (Pick 3.)**

9. For each of your three incongruent areas, what you could do to become more congruent. Select one you can commit to addressing immediately.

10. What kinds of clients do you love working with?

11. How can you attract more of these clients to your practice?

12. What kinds of clients make you groan inside when you see them on the schedule?

13. What might you be doing to draw these clients to your practice? How can you attract fewer of these clients to your practice?

14. What professional image do you think you currently project?

15. What professional image would you like to project?

16. How can your marketing efforts reinforce this professional image?

17. What personal image do you think you currently project? (How do you present yourself?)

18. What things could you improve upon in your personal presentation?

19. Go to your office and pretend that you're a new patient. Walk in through the front doors and tour your office. What do you see? Hear? Smell? Do all of these things combine to create the best presentation of your office? What could you improve upon?

29

20. Review all of the forms your patients complete. What do they look like? Do they represent your image accurately? What can you improve upon?

21. **What is your personal reputation? Your professional reputation? Better yet, create and send out a survey as described in chapter 2 of *Community Connections!* and find out!**

22. **Do you have a set fee for each of your services, or does it change with the patient or situation?**

23. Do you and your staff know your fees? Do you have a fee schedule available for clients?

24. Do you feel your fees are appropriate? If you haven't looked at them in some time (or if you're not sure), contact your state association, professional organizations, and/or local colleagues to see what is the average in your area.

25. What is your marketing comfort zone? Put another way, what are your marketing preferences and limits? (For example, perhaps you love to give presentations to small mother's groups, but you are too nervous to give a presentation to more than 10 people at a time.) Spend some time on this and really explore your boundaries.

26. What do you do to actively improve yourself personally?

27. What do you do to actively improve yourself professionally?

28. If money is no problem, there are NO barriers, and you're guaranteed to succeed…what does your *ideal* practice look like? Describe it in as vivid detail as you possibly can. Add diagrams, drawings, pictures, brand names, and anything else that makes it more concrete. What does it look like? How is it laid out? What kinds of patients are there? How many patients are there? How many employees work in this practice and what are their personalities like? What does the parking lot look like? Do you have plants inside? What sounds do you hear? What can you smell? Et cetera. Consider making a vision board with this information.

Chapter 3: Do You Understand Your Communities?

1. **What are the demographics of your geographic community? (If you don't know…look them up!)**
   a. Local population and the population including surrounding townships (In other words…we're looking at your potential patient pool…)
   b. Median age, income, education level
   c. Percentage & numbers of men and women
   d. How many kids?

2. Given the numbers, what are the healthcare *needs* of this area?

3. How can your practice meet the needs and desires of the geographic community you serve? (Be specific!)

4. **What is currently being done to support wellness in this area? What can you do to raise awareness and facilitate?**

5. **How can you give back to the community?**

6. **What are your best networking opportunities in this geographic community?**
   a. **What relationships develop naturally?**
   b. **Where (or who) are your best opportunities for cross-referrals?**

7. **What are the demographics of your *healthcare* community?**
   a. **Types of providers**
   b. **Numbers of each type of provider**
   c. **Is your healthcare community more allopathic or holistic?**

8. **How can you support and give back to your healthcare community?**

9. **What are your best networking opportunities within your healthcare community?**

10. Where are your best opportunities for cross-referrals?

11. How can you help other healthcare professionals prosper?

12. Make a list of people in your *personal* community who aren't part of your geographic or healthcare communities.

   a. How can you best communicate your skills and services to them?

   b. What are their health needs and concerns?

Part 2:
Connecting vs. Marketing

Chapter 4: Community Connections

1. When you first saw the term "relationship marketing," what did you think it meant?

2. Now that you've read *Community Connections!,* how has your perception of relationship marketing changed?

3. **What are some ways in which your office already exemplifies a patient-centered practice?**

4. **In what areas could your office improve and become more patient-centered?**

45

5. **In what ways could you improve your patient-centered focus?**

6. **What is the hardest thing for you about trying to explain a diagnosis or condition to your patients?**

7. Do you feel you're able to present medical terms in common language so your patients easily understand their conditions? In what ways could you improve your communication?

8. Are you – or one of your employees – fluent in another language? If so, how can that be useful in your practice?

9. Is there a large population of non-English speaking people in your community? How could you better communicate with them?

10. When you make a recommendation to a patient, and they ignore your advice, how does that make you feel?

11. Do you feel you care more about your patient's health than they do?

12. How could you detach yourself from your patient's choices?

13. At what point (if any) would you decide to sever your relationship with a patient who was not following your instructions? Could you do anything to prevent the situation from getting to that point?

14. How can you balance your professional experience, knowledge, and training with a patient's opinion of what's going on in their body?

15. What are specific ways in which you can demonstrate you're actively listening to your patients? (If you're not familiar with this term, you may want to Google it before you respond.) Place a checkmark next to those behaviors you already exhibit…and a star next to the top three you'd like to develop.

16. Have you ever had a patient whose personality clashed with yours? One you simply didn't like? If so, how did you handle the situation?

www.DrKelleyPendleton.com

17. Imagine a new patient comes into your office and your personalities are like oil and water. You know she won't be happy in your office…and that she'll drain your energy. You decide the best thing for everyone is to not accept her as a patient and refer her to a colleague you feel would be a better match. Describe how you could communicate this to her in a professional and compassionate way.

18. Have you ever had a time where you didn't feel up to seeing patients (physically or emotionally)? How did you handle it? Was this the best approach for all involved?

19. **What is the average time a patient waits in your reception area, consultation room, exam room, and / or treatment room? How would you feel if you were the patient?**

20. **In what areas can you streamline your processes and procedures to reduce the wait time experienced by your patients?**

21. Do you have patients from different cultures? If so, do you understand their culture's basic beliefs and ideas about health and healthcare?

22. Think of a time when someone was not genuine with you. How did it make you feel?

23. Have you ever not been genuine with your patients? Why? How can you turn this around?

24. Are you considered to be a leader in your community?

25. **How do you serve your communities?**

26. **Are you reliable, dependable, and honest? Would your family and friends agree, or do you need to work on these areas?**

27. Are you passionate about your profession? If not – were you ever passionate about your profession? How can you regain your passion?

28. Do you have a vision for your life and your practice? (If not, develop one.)

29. Do you feel confident and competent in your professional skill sets? If not, list 10 ways you can improve upon these areas.

30. Does the fear of failure ever paralyze you?

31. Describe a situation where you initially felt you failed, but it had a very positive outcome.

Chapter 5: Marketing 101 – The Basics

1. **What types of external marketing do you currently do in your practice?**

2. **What types if internal marketing do you currently do in your practice?**

3. **Does your office have an on-line presence?**

4. **What on-ground marketing activities does your office do?**

5. **What are your short-term marketing activities?**

6. What are your long-term marketing activities?

7. Do you complete a written marketing calendar every year?

Chapter 6: Your Connections Calendar™

1. **What date(s) have you set aside to create your Connections Calendar™?**

2. **Where will you create your Connections Calendar™?**

3. **Will you create a digital or printed Connections Calendar™?**

4. **What aspirations do you have for your goal-setting day(s)?**

5. **What material(s) will you be bringing with you?**

6. **Who else will be involved in the creation of your Connections Calendar™ and how will they be involved?**

7. **Do you have a "signature" marketing event? If so, please describe it. If not, is there an event you would like to become your signature event?**

8. **What feedback have you received from your patients regarding previous marketing efforts? (If your answer is "none, please consider a client survey as discussed in Chapter 6!)"**

9. **What vacations or other special events will you need to schedule around?**

10. What 12 internal events and 12 external events would you like to do next year?

11. **For each of the above events, write down your goals for that event. (For example, 3 new patients; raise $1,500 for M.A.D.D.; increase community awareness about autism; et cetera.)**

12. What are the benefits of achieving each goal?

13. What are the consequences of falling short on each goal?

71

14. What is the time frame for each goal?

15. How will you measure each goal?

73

16. What skills or resources will you need to reach each goal?

74

17. Are there any possible roadblocks for each goal? If so, what are they and how can you work around them?

18. How will you track your results for each event?

19. How will you organize your digital or physical Connections Calendar™ materials? (Try listing the items in outline format – then you can use this outline to create your actual tracking materials.)

20. How can you communicate your plan for each event to key people?

21. How will show appreciation to your staff, volunteers, and participants in your events?

22. Select one marketing event or activity you did in the past which was "unsuccessful." Why was it unsuccessful? What could be done differently in the future to make it a resounding success for your practice?

23. Select one marketing event or activity you did in the past which was "successful." Why was it successful? How can you apply this to other marketing events to make them successful as well? (Write down as many things as you can here!)

Congratulations on completing this workbook! I hope it enhances your productivity and launches your practice to new levels. Don't stop here. Stay motivated. Plan. Take action, and modify as needed. If you have questions, comments, or would just like to share your story, I'd love to hear from you!

Email me at DrKelley@DrKelleyPendleton.com

If you haven't already, please check out my books or submit a review through your favorite major online retailer.

Community Connections!
Relationship Marketing for Healthcare Professionals

Whether you're a chiropractor, medical doctor, massage therapist, veterinarian, acupuncturist, or any other provider of a healing art, the healthcare industry is rapidly changing. If you want to connect with your community and achieve greater success, marketing is a must—a fact that has unfortunately been overlooked in many health-related fields of study.

But why don't many independent healthcare professionals tend to actively market their services? And how can self-awareness help you forge a genuine relationship with potential clients?

These questions and more are addressed in *Community Connections!*, a valuable guide full of ideas for marketing your independent healthcare practice effectively and easily.

Coming Soon!

Practice Excellence!
An Integrated Approach to Creating a World-Class Healthcare Practice

In our current healthcare climate, more providers are choosing to run their own *independent* practices instead of being affiliated with a larger group or hospital. As the second book in a series, **Practice Excellence!** picks up where **Community Connections!** left off – helping healthcare practices of all disciplines to market smarter, not harder.

What is *Practice Excellence*? How do you build a professional team and your "A-Team?" What statistics must you track to take the "pulse" of your practice? And what critical marketing can you do while you're within the four walls of your practice?

These questions and more are addressed in *Practice Excellence!*, a valuable guide full of ideas for building and marketing your independent healthcare practice effectively and easily.

Author Biography

Dr. Kelley Pendleton graduated from Logan College of Chiropractic in 2005 with a Doctorate of Chiropractic. She also holds Master's degrees in Public Health and Alternative Dispute Resolution, as well as Bachelor's degrees in Psychology, Sociology, and Human Biology.

For more than ten years, she has worked in the healthcare industry in various capacities—as an employee, business owner, mentor, healthcare marketing consultant, professional speaker, and educator. When Dr. Pendleton first entered private practice, she couldn't find a book with marketing ideas appropriate for an independent healthcare business. This struggle provided the inspiration for the *Community Connections* series. She hopes this series will serve as a road map for healthcare practitioners working to build the practice and community of their dreams.

She currently lives in Mandeville, Louisiana, with her fiancé, Michael, and their two furry, four-legged children: Cree and Suki.